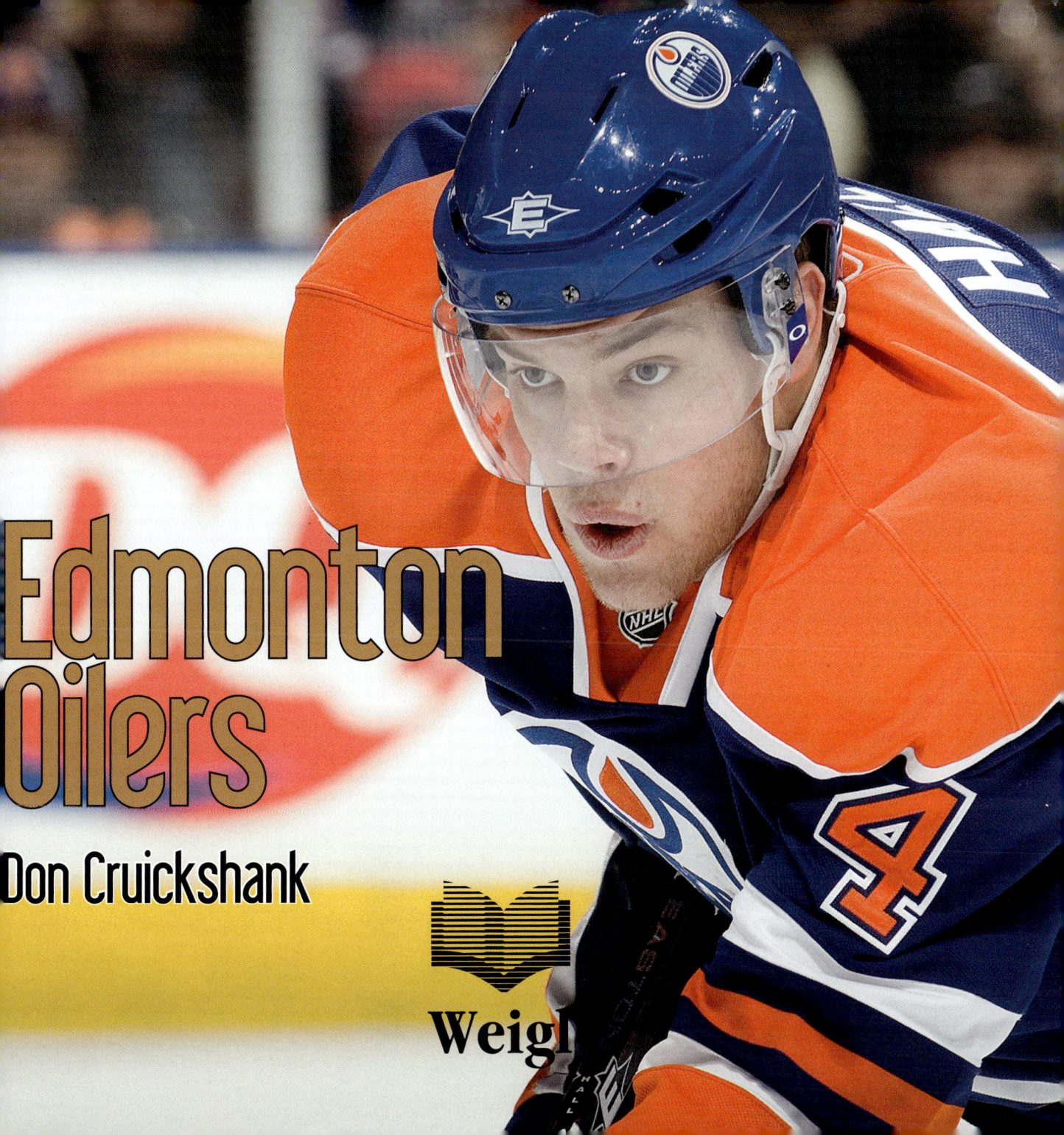

Edmonton
Oilers

Don Cruickshank

Weigl

The publisher wishes to thank the Hoffart Family for inspiring this series.

Published by Weigl Educational Publishers Limited
6325 10th Street SE
Calgary, AB T2H 2Z9
Website: www.weigl.ca

Library and Archives Canada Cataloguing in Publication
Cruickshank, Don, 1977-
          Edmonton Oilers / Don Cruickshank.

(Hockey in Canada)
Includes index.
ISBN 978-1-77071-641-4 (bound).--ISBN 978-1-77071-655-1 (pbk.)

          1. Edmonton Oilers (Hockey team)--Juvenile literature.
I. Title. II. Series: Cruickshank, Don, 1977- . Hockey in Canada.
GV848.E35C775 2011   j796.962'6409712334   C2011-900789-4

Printed in the United States of America in North Mankato, Minnesota
1 2 3 4 5 6 7 8 9 0 15 14 13 12 11

072011
WEP040711

Project Coordinator Aaron Carr
Art Director Terry Paulhus

Weigl acknowledges Getty Images as its primary image supplier for this title.

Every reasonable effort has been made to trace ownership and to obtain
permission to reprint copyright material. The publisher would be pleased
to have any errors or omissions brought to their attention so they may be
corrected in subsequent printings.

We acknowledge the financial support of the Government of Canada through
the Canada Book Fund for our publishing activities.

CONTENTS

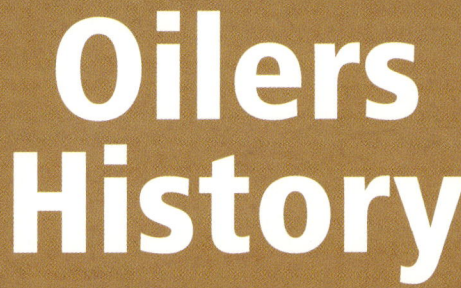

Oilers History

The Edmonton Oilers started as a professional hockey team in the World Hockey Association (WHA) in 1972. The WHA **folded** in 1979. That year, the Oilers were one of four WHA teams to join the **National Hockey League (NHL)**.

During the 1980s, the Oilers won the **Stanley Cup** five times in seven seasons. The team set many records. This success helped earn Edmonton the nickname, "City of Champions."

The Oilers won their first Stanley Cup in 1984. In total, they have won the cup five times.

Home Arena

The Oilers first home **arena** was called the Edmonton Gardens. It was built in 1913 and was the first indoor hockey arena in Edmonton. The Gardens was a small arena with a **capacity** of 5,200 people. After two seasons, the Oilers moved to the Northlands Coliseum.

The new arena could hold about 17,000 fans during Oilers games. This is the building they play in today. Its current name is Rexall Place.

There are **23 championship banners** hanging from the roof of Rexall Place.

The Jerseys

The home jersey is blue with white and orange trim. It is the same jersey worn in Edmonton's first NHL season.

The away jersey is white. The **logo** is the same as the home jersey, except it has copper trim instead of orange.

The third jersey is similar to the away jersey, except the main colour is dark blue instead of white.

The third jersey from 2001 to 2007 was created by comic book artist Todd McFarlane.

Goalie Masks

 Grant Fuhr was the Oilers goalie for most of the 1980s. His mask was painted with Edmonton's team colours.

 Bill Ranford helped the Oilers win their last Stanley Cup in 1990. His mask was painted with blue and orange oil drops.

 Dwayne Roloson and the Oilers played for the Stanley Cup in 2006. "Roli," his nickname, was painted on the chin.

Devan Dubnyk has an outdoor pond hockey game painted on his mask.

The Coaches

 Glen Sather was the Oilers first coach in the NHL. He was behind the bench for 11 seasons and won 426 games.

 John Muckler was the Oilers head coach for two years. He coached the Oilers to the Stanley Cup in 1990.

 Craig MacTavish played nine seasons with the Oilers. He later served as the coach from 2000 to 2009.

Tom Renney became the 10th coach in Oilers team history in 2010.

Dance Team

The Oilers are one of four teams in the NHL that do not have a **mascot**. Instead, Edmonton has cheerleaders. This cheerleading squad started near the start of the 2010–2011 season. They are called the Oilers Octane dance team. There are 19 members in the team.

The Oilers Octane leads the crowd in cheers during home games. They also attend many events in the community.

The Oilers are the first NHL team in Canada to have cheerleaders.

Oilers Records

OILERS ALL-TIME LEADERS

Most Goals
Wayne Gretzky
583 goals

Most Games Played
Kevin Lowe
1,037 games played

Most Penalty Minutes
Kelly Buchberger
1,747 penalty minutes

Most Assists
Wayne Gretzky
1,086 assists

Most Points
Wayne Gretzky
1,669 points

Most Goaltender Wins
Grant Fuhr
226 wins

Legendary
Oilers

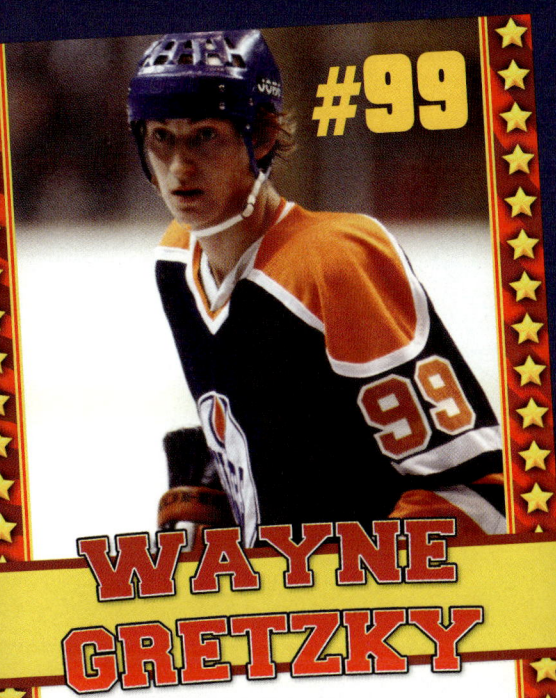

#99

WAYNE GRETZKY

Position: Centre
Seasons with Oilers: 9
Born: January 26, 1961
Hometown: Brantford, Ontario

CAREER FACTS

Wayne Gretzky was captain of the Oilers when they won the Stanley Cup in 1984, 1985, 1987, and 1988. Gretzky's nickname is "The Great One." He led the league in scoring 10 times and was named the NHL's **Most Valuable Player (MVP)** nine times. In 1,487 career NHL games, he scored 894 goals and 1,963 assists, for 2,857 total points. These are all NHL records. Gretzky retired in 1999 and was inducted into the **Hockey Hall of Fame**.

#11

MARK MESSIER

Position: Centre
Seasons with Oilers: 12
Born: January 18, 1961
Hometown: Edmonton, Alberta

CAREER FACTS

Mark Messier was captain of the Oilers when they won the Stanley Cup in 1990. He was awarded the Conn Smythe Trophy as the MVP of the playoffs in 1984. Messier also won the Hart Trophy as the NHL's regular season MVP in 1990 and 1992. In 1,756 career NHL games, Messier recorded 694 goals and 1,193 assists, for a total of 1,887 points. This ranks him second on the all-time scoring list.

Star
Oilers

#4

TAYLOR HALL

Position: Left Wing
Seasons with Oilers: 1
Born: November 14, 1991
Hometown: Calgary, Alberta

CAREER FACTS

Taylor Hall was the first pick in the 2010 **NHL entry draft**. He started playing for the Oilers when he was 18 years old. In his **rookie** season, Hall scored 22 goals and 20 assists in 65 games played. Hall was leading the Oilers in goals before he sprained his ankle and was forced to miss the rest of the season. He missed the last 17 games of the season, but he still finished the year as one of the top 10 rookie scorers in the league.

#14

JORDAN EBERLE

Position: Right Wing
Seasons with Oilers: 1
Born: May 15, 1990
Hometown: Regina, Saskatchewan

CAREER FACTS

Eberle holds the record for most all-time goals for Team Canada at the World Junior Hockey Championships, with 14. He was the Oilers' first-round pick in the 2008 draft. In his first NHL season in 2010–2011, Eberle became one of the top players in Edmonton. That season, Eberle scored 18 goals and 25 assists. His 43 points were the sixth best among all NHL rookies.

Unforgettable Moments

1980

In their first NHL season, the Oilers make the playoffs. This year, Wayne Gretzky becomes the youngest player in NHL history to score 100 points in a season.

1988

Gretzky is traded from Edmonton to the Los Angeles Kings. He later finishes his career as a member of the New York Rangers in 1999.

2003

The Oilers and Montreal Canadiens play the first NHL outdoor game. It is called the Heritage Classic. About 57,000 fans watch the game as the temperature drops to −30 °Celsius. The Oilers lose 4–3.

1984

The Oilers finish the season in first place in the overall league standings, with 119 points. This is the first of two times the Oilers end the regular season as the best team in the NHL. The Oilers win their first Stanley Cup this year. It is the first time a team from western Canada had won the cup since the Victoria Cougars in 1925.

2006

The Oilers reach the Stanley Cup final for the first time since 1990. They end up losing the series to the Carolina Hurricanes in seven games.

Brain Teasers

Test your knowledge of the Edmonton Oilers by trying to answer these brain teasers.

1. How many times have the Edmonton Oilers won the Stanley Cup?

2. What is the name of the Oilers cheerleading team?

3. What team did the Oilers play in the NHL's first outdoor game?

4. What is the name of the arena where the Oilers play their home games?

5. Which Oilers player has scored the most goals?

ANSWERS: 1. Five 2. The Oilers Octane 3. Montreal Canadiens 4. Rexall Place 5. Wayne Gretzky

Glossary

arena: a building where sports teams play their games

capacity: the maximum number of people that can fit in a stadium

folded: went out of business

Hockey Hall of Fame: a place where people involved in hockey are honoured for their efforts

logo: a symbol that identifies a team

mascot: an animal or object used to bring a team good luck

Most Valuable Player (MVP): the player judged to be the most important to his team's success

National Hockey League (NHL): an organization for professional hockey teams

NHL entry draft: when NHL teams select junior hockey players to join their organizations

rookie: a player in his or her first season

Stanley Cup: the National Hockey League's prize for the best team in the playoffs

Index